MY VERY OWN JEWISH HOME

written by

Rabbi Andrew Goldstein

photographs by

Madeline Wikler

KAR-BEN COPIES, INC.   ROCKVILLE, MD

Library of Congress Cataloging in Publication Data

Goldstein, Andrew, 1943—
  My very own Jewish home.

  Summary: In text and photos, a young girl identifies the objects that
make her home a Jewish one.
  1. Jewish way of life—Juvenile literature.
[1. Jews—United States] I. Wikler, Madeline, 1943-
ill. II. Title.
BM723.G64   1983   296.4   83-4357
ISBN 0-930494-24-5
ISBN 0-930494-08-3 (pbk.)

Second Printing, 1983

Printed in the United States of America.

FOREWORD

With the publication of *My Very Own Jewish Home*, Kar-Ben Copies has gone international.

We are delighted to introduce our readers to Andrew Goldstein, Rabbi of the Northwood and Pinner Liberal Synagogue in London, England. Rabbi Goldstein has shared the "My Very Own" holiday books with families and children in his congregation across the Atlantic.

During a recent sabbatical, he and his wife Sharon and children Ruth and Aaron spent Sukkot with the Kar-Ben families. We shared ideas for new books, and encouraged Rabbi Goldstein to work with us.

He wrote *My Very Own Jewish Home* to help young children begin to build a Jewish identity through an awareness of the Jewish objects in their environment. The presence of Jewish objects does not make a home Jewish. We tried, therefore, to talk about how the objects are used in Shabbat and holiday celebration, and hope our readers will do the same.

Our special thanks to Karen Wikler, for her patience and enthusiasm through countless photographic sessions.

From the end of my street
all the houses look like mine.
There are bikes in the driveways
and flowers in the gardens.

But when we get to my house
there is a difference.
My house is a Jewish house.

We know it is a Jewish house
even before we go inside.

There is a mezuzah
on the doorpost.
I can hardly reach it.

My dad told me we
put it there
to remind us
of God and His
commandments.

Our mezuzah is clay, and the scroll inside is very tiny. It is made of parchment, just like the parchment used to make the Torah.

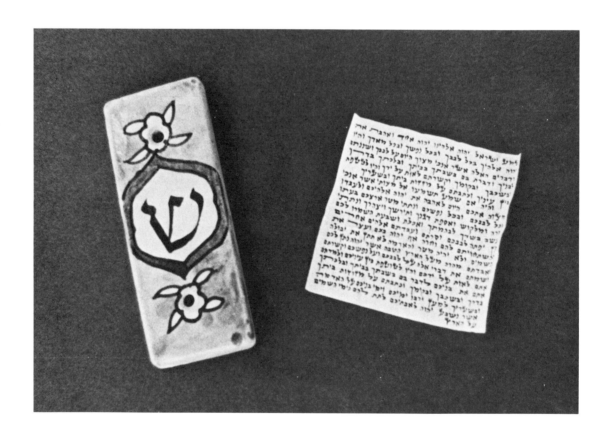

On the parchment a scribe has written the words of the Shema, which tells us there is One God.

Come inside my
house. There are lots
of things that make it
Jewish. I bet some of
them are in your
house, too.

This is my living room. We have a whole wall of bookshelves where we keep our most important Jewish books.

Next to the prayer books is our Bible. I know it is a Jewish Bible because it has English on one side of the page and Hebrew on the other. We have many copies of the Pesach Haggadah, so everyone at the Seder can have one.

I like the big books with photos
about Israel the best.

There are lots of other Jewish books, but they are too hard for me. When I asked my parents why we have so many books, my mom smiled and said that the Jewish people are called "The People of the Book."

I guess that is why I like to read so much.

Our dining room is quiet all week, but on Shabbat and the holidays it is the busiest and most Jewish room in the house.

I help set the table
for holiday meals
with the candlesticks, the kiddush cups,
and the challah cover I made myself.

I love the braided candle we light on Saturday night to say good-bye to Shabbat. But when I sniff the spice box, sometimes I sneeze.

We have two Chanukah menorahs.
One is made of clay, and my parents light
it. The other is made of wood.

Guess who made it?
I did, and I am allowed to light it
all eight nights.

Except for my room, the kitchen is my favorite. There is a lot in here that tells us we are in a Jewish home. Sometimes I can close my eyes and know just by the smell that a Jewish holiday is coming up.

We have piles of cookbooks. Yogurt ones, French ones, bread ones and diet ones. But the ones with the messiest covers and most worn pages are our Jewish cookbooks.

I like to cook, but I love to bake.
Best of all is kneading bread dough
and twisting it for challah.

We don't always have home-made challah,
but when we do,
it is as much fun making it
as eating it.

I always make
a little one just for me.

Baking cookies is fun, too, especially when we use our Chanukah and Purim cookie cutters. There is always dough left over for me to taste.

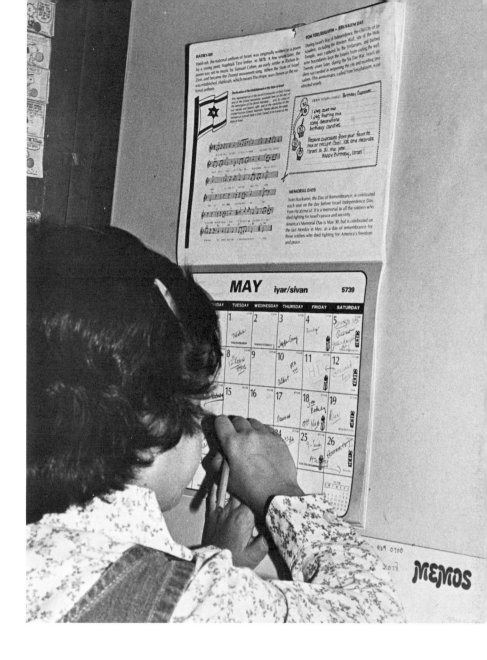

On the wall over the telephone
is a Jewish calendar.
It is like any other calendar,
but it also shows the Hebrew
dates and Jewish holidays.

There are Jewish things in my parents' room, too. Dad keeps his tallit and kippah in his dresser.

Our photo albums are in the closet. When I am sick and cannot go to school, I love to look through them. There are pictures of me when I was a baby, pictures of my brother's Bar Mitzvah, and pictures of my great-grandparents who came from Poland. I like to hear stories about them.

But my very favorite pictures are from my parents' wedding. Daddy looks very young and kind of funny.

I saved the best room—mine—for last. I have lots of stuff, so you may not be able to tell at first that mine is a Jewish room, too.

I have a shell collection, 19 stuffed animals, and a goldfish named Abraham.

I have a shelf of books and
records, and some of them are Jewish.
There is a book of Jewish songs,
and I can play the easy ones on
the piano. I have my own
Haggadah, a book of Jewish crafts,
Bible stories, and my own prayer book.

The book bag on the floor is not really Jewish, but I keep my Hebrew school books in it, and I call it my Jewish bag.

Some of my Jewish toys were presents, and others I made myself. I have lots of dreidles. One came filled with candy, but it is empty now. My grogger is super noisy. It is filled with bottle caps and dried beans, and when I shake it, my dad says it gives him a headache.

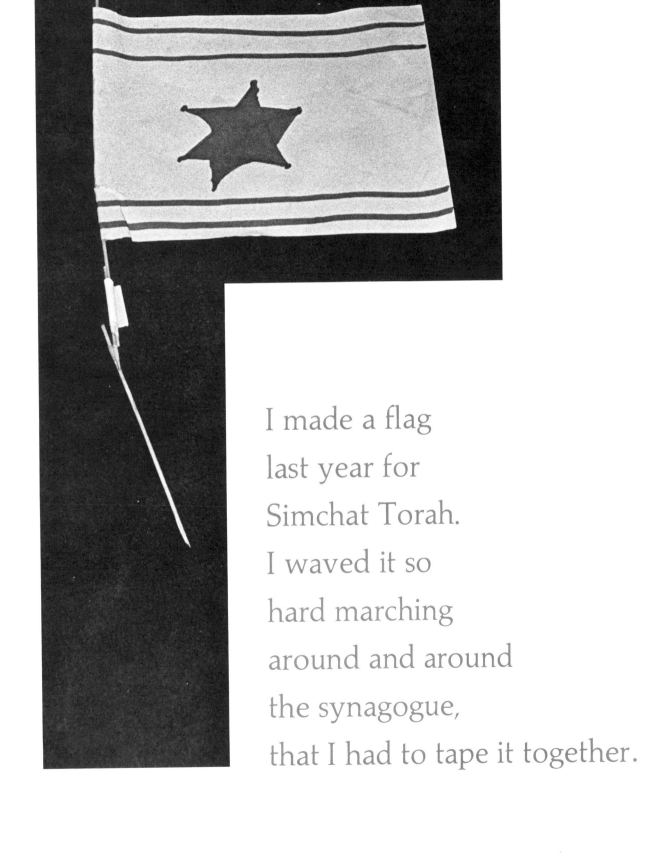

I made a flag
last year for
Simchat Torah.
I waved it so
hard marching
around and around
the synagogue,
that I had to tape it together.

My tzedakah box is on the dresser. I put part of my allowance in it every week. When Grandpa comes, he lets me search all of his pockets for pennies to put in there, too.

On the wall over my bed is the certificate I got for planting a tree in Israel last Tu B'Shevat. I took the money from my tzedakah box. I wonder how big my tree is now.

One week every year, on Sukkot, we have a Jewish backyard. I am in charge of decorating our sukkah. We string paper chains and

hang all kinds of fruit. I put our New Year's cards and some of my artwork on the walls. We move our picnic table into the sukkah, and I even eat breakfast there.

But I almost forgot
the most important thing that
makes mine a Jewish home...

The people in it!

Even without any of the Jewish objects, it would still be a Jewish home, because we are a Jewish family.

Everybody's home is different. What kind of Jewish objects can you find in yours?

KAR-BEN COPIES PUBLICATIONS

My Very Own Rosh Hashanah
My Very Own Yom Kippur
My Very Own Sukkot
My Very Own Simchat Torah
My Very Own Chanukah
My Very Own Megillah
My Very Own Haggadah
My Very Own Shavuot
My Very Own Jewish Calendar
Come, Let Us Welcome Shabbat
        by Judyth R. Saypol and Madeline Wikler

Let's Celebrate — 57 Holiday Crafts
Let's Have A Party
        by Ruth Esrig Brinn

Only Nine Chairs — A Tall Tale
Poppy Seeds, Too — A Twisted Tale
        by Deborah Miller and Karen Ostrove

The Mouse in the Matzah Factory
        by Francine Medoff and David Goldstein

The Children We Remember
        by Chana Byers Abells

My Very Own Jewish Home
        by Andrew Goldstein and Madeline Wikler

Holiday Adventures of Achbar
        by Barbara Sofer and Nina Gaelen

Mi Ani — Who Am I?
        by Rochelle Sobel and Meir Pluznick